Christians Who Will Not Be Saved!

Christians Who <u>*Will Not*</u> Be Saved!

John Elliott Williams

Jesus said, "Because narrow is the gate and difficult is the way which leads to life and there are few who find it" Matthew 7:14 NKJV.

"And Jesus said, "I do not know you!"

While they went to buy, the bridegroom came, and those who were ready went in with him to the wedding; and the door was shut. "Afterward the other virgins came also, saying, 'Lord, Lord, open to us!' But he answered and said, 'Assuredly, I say to you, I do not know you" Matthew 25:10-12 (NKJV).

INTRODUCTION

O ne of the strangest conversation for believers to have is
discussing the *fact* that a multitude of Christians _will not be saved!_
Not only is it strange, it is true, and it is validated by Scripture. In His
parables, Jesus Christ revealed the down-fall of His followers *(the
multitude)*. He prophesied their fate, as well as the destiny of today's
Christians. As faithful believers, we should read and understand
Jesus' parables as though He is speaking directly to us!

He revealed many secrets that can sustain our lives and deliver us
from the enemy. Therefore, as members of His body, we now have the
knowledge to make wise choices in the fulfillment of God's
predestination plan for our lives. This spiritual phenomenon can only
occur if the Holy Spirit imparts to us wisdom from above and gives
the understanding we need.

In His teachings, Jesus spoke of the mysteries of God's Kingdom
which reveals the following: Truth regarding the mixture in the
church as spoken by Jesus in the parable of the wheat and tares; the
infiltration of false ministers; and how the weakness of human flesh in
the Christian affects our course in life. For our eternal benefit, He also
gave us the signs of the end of the age that reveal the devastation that
will occur prior to His return.

While illustrating these tragedies, Jesus gives a clear revelation of
those who will receive eternal life. Because of these spiritual
happenings, there is still much to learn; but remember, insight to
these Scriptures and of God's Word only comes alive to us by the

Spirit! We must not solely depend on our spiritual leaders for direction because oftentimes they are unlearned themselves. After their maturity in the Spirit, most of Jesus' apostles spoke of the false teaching that would occur in the household of faith and warned the body of Christ of its pitfalls.

Open your eyes and see that the mixture spoken of has already occurred in the household of faith. Not all Christians respond to God's Word the same! Many take God's Word lightly to fulfill the lusts of their flesh which either grieves or quenches the Holy Spirit. Practicing the works of their flesh violates God's Word. Nevertheless, God's Word is true and will not return to Him void! "So shall My word be that goes forth from My mouth; it shall not return to Me void, but it shall accomplish what I please, and it shall prosper in the thing for which I sent it" Isaiah 55:11(NKJV). It will render to all, the choice to receive this truth and obey it or face damnation! God already has a people who has surrendered their hearts to Jesus and are living according to God's Spirit. Still, there are some who are spiritually blind to the things of God and live according to their flesh.

Therefore, at the wedding feast, many of God's people will hear Jesus say, "Verily I say unto you, I know you not!" Now is the time to make that spiritual change in your life, remembering the words of our Lord: "Watch therefore, for you know neither the day nor the hour in which the Son of Man is coming" Matthew 25:13(NKJV).

CONTENTS

Introduction

A Final Word from the Author

CHAPTER ONE

God's Spirit Battles Human Flesh!

In the parable of the sower, Jesus tells us about many of His followers who cannot see nor hear spiritually. This happens because of the dullness of their hearts. In the parable of the wheat and tares found in the book of Matthews of the New Testament, Jesus warns us about the mixture *(wheat and tares)* in the church and how Satan has sowed tares *(wicked people)* in the mist of the wheat *(faithful believers)*. These tares are both ministers and congregants. Jesus further revealed the infiltration of false worshippers and religious leaders by stating, "These people draw near to Me with their mouth, and honor Me with their lips, but their heart is far from Me. And in vain they worship Me, teaching as doctrines the commandments of men" Matthew 15:8-9(NKJV).

As Christians seeking God's Kingdom, we must take to heart all Scriptures and their meanings because at the end of this age, they will save our lives from eternal damnation. Born as sinful flesh, our hearts become wicked which cause us to need God's Word to transform us into righteous beings?

This will occur only if we allow the Word of God to perform its work. "For the word of God is alive and powerful. It is sharper than the sharpest two-edged sword, cutting between soul and spirit, between joint and marrow. It exposes our innermost thoughts and desires" Hebrews 4:12 (NLT). By exposing our innermost thoughts and desires, God gives us the chance to make wise decisions based on the truth of His Word. His Spirit can change the rudiments of our hearts by influencing a change in our thoughts and desires, leading us into righteousness.

"The law of Moses was _unable_ to save us because of the weakness of our sinful nature. God did what the law could not do. He sent his own Son in a human form like the bodies we sinners have. And in that body, God declared an end to sin's control over us by giving his Son as the perfect sacrifice for our sins. He did this so that the requirement of the law would be fully satisfied for us, and we would _no longer follow_ our sinful nature but instead follow the Spirit" Romans 8:3-4 (NLT). Believers must be Spirit-filled and mature to _even_ understand and discern these Scriptures that can change our lives, particularly the Word regarding life in God's Kingdom.

Jesus parables unveil the mysteries of God's Kingdom that _only_ Spirit-filled faithful believers can comprehend. Hence, we must seek God's Kingdom and His righteousness. If we learn the secrets of God's Kingdom and obey them, we will achieve God's predestination plan to become sons and daughters adopted through our acceptance of Jesus Christ and living according to the guidance of the Holy Spirit! Are you aware that this is the reason for our existence? God created us to become His children and our earthly experience is the testing ground to determine who will fulfill God's Plan. Many of God's mysteries and secrets, made-known by Jesus Christ, in His parables are designed to accomplish this end.

To spiritually qualify ourselves to hear from above, we must _crucify_ our flesh so that we do not grieve or quench the Holy Spirit. Crucifying our flesh means we put to death the lust and desires of our sinful nature. This is the only way we can receive spiritual insight and discernment from the Holy Spirit! "And those who are Christ's have crucified the flesh with its passions and desires" Galatians 5:24(NKJV). As born-again Christians, we can resist the temptations that arise within us! You may hear people say that they have good *will power*. *Will power* is a carnal expression that simply means to restrain impulses. Generally, most people can only restrain their impulses for a short period of time. In reality, will power is not considered total deliverance! So, the battle goes on and on and on.

Total deliverance, on the other hand, comes from and through God's Spirit. The Holy Spirit works in the heart of the believer, as well as in the believer's mind. If we truly desire deliverance from a known vice or sin, we must pray and ask the Lord to deliver us. Only then will God's Spirit intervene on our behalf. However, the reason a multitude of Christians do not experience true deliverance is because they seek the wrong things. So many Christians are praying and seeking to reward the appetites of their flesh. I will expound further. As mentioned above, our flesh is weak, and it desires pleasure and worldly gains instead of deliverance from the enemy.

James uncovered the real battle of our flesh when he said, "You lust and do not have. You murder and covet and cannot obtain. You fight and war. Yet you do not have because you do not ask. You ask and do not receive, because you ask amiss *(incorrect or inappropriate)*, that you may spend it on *your pleasures*" James 4:2-3(NKJV). Human flesh has a tendency to pray for material things or things that gratify *(pleases, delight, satisfy or thrill)* our flesh.

Even as Christians, our flesh desires more of everything; moreover, all humans seem to have great difficulty in being satisfied with just enough. If God blesses us with a four-room house, we want an eight-room house. He gives us a Honda; we want a Lexus. He gives you a good and faithful spouse, you still find something wrong with him or her. The Holy Spirit comes to deliver us from these natural urges *(impulses, longing, wish or desires)* that keep us in bondage. His power undergirds the believer in overcoming the sins of this world. He also draws us closer to God by our study of Scriptures.

It is extremely important for God's Spirit to enable faithful believers to hear, to see and to understand the things of God. Jesus' parables give useful instruction to true believers on how to walk to be saved. However, the believer must be Spirit-filled and spiritually sound to know and understand the words Jesus speaks. Believers must acknowledge the Holy Spirit. Please do not be deceived! Understand the fate of those who allow the *lust of their flesh* to rule their heart. These individuals go through the motion of Christianity, but they bare little or no fruit. They neither hear nor understand the things God's Spirit is saying.

The first thing Jesus told His disciples when they inquired about the end of time was to take heed that no one deceives them. He wanted them to use their spiritual knowledge and understanding to discern the things they had heard and seen from His teachings. Christians must do likewise to hear the voice of God's Spirit. Jesus wants us to rely on His teachings of God's Kingdom and its mysteries. However, a multitude of Jesus followers did not understand the revelation of God's Kingdom just like multitudes today do not understand its mysteries and secrets! I cannot say enough that the parables *(mysteries)* require spiritual understanding and discernment to know the truth of Jesus' teachings. Once Jesus' disciples grew in maturity, they understood His teachings by the Spirit and so shall we!

Understanding the mysteries of God's Kingdom gives clarity to the end of time and to other situations and even events that happen in our lifetime. This truth avails itself particularly to those who seek salvation. One popular prophecy, given by Jesus, is the parable of the wise and foolish virgins. This parable explains future events that will occur at the end of the age when the bridegroom *(Jesus)* is delayed. Read it by the Spirit and do not be deceived of its truth regarding Christian behavior preceding Christ's return to gather his saints. It illustrates how some _born-again Christians_ are allowing themselves to be influenced by the things of this world to a level that quenches God's Spirit. Consequently, many believers are avoiding the fulfillment of their gifts and calling from God to satisfy the desires of their flesh.

The garden experience proves to us that God's people can be indwelled with His Spirit and still allow the lust of their flesh to dominate the choices they make in life. Such was the case with Eve in the Garden of Eden. She was in a close relationship with God which is symbolic of today's Christians being indwelled with the Holy Spirit. Unfortunately, Eve allowed her flesh to lust after the tree for food. Then she chose the forbidden fruit on the tree to eat rather than obey God's Word to Adam not to eat fruit of this tree. "So when the woman saw that the tree was *good* for food, that it was *pleasant* to the eyes, and a tree *desirable* to make one wise, she took of its fruit and ate. She also gave to her husband with her, and he ate" Genesis 3:6 (NKJV). This is one of the reasons the Holy Spirit battles our flesh daily. Both desire to take the control of our souls!

Living by the Power of God's Spirit!

"So, I say, let the Holy Spirit guide your lives. Then you won't be doing what your sinful nature craves. The sinful nature wants to do evil, which is just the opposite of what the Spirit wants. And the Spirit gives us desires that are the opposite of what the sinful nature desires. These two forces are

constantly fighting each other, _so you are not free to carry out your good intentions. But when you are directed by the Spirit, you are not under obligation to the Law of Moses" Galatians 5:16-18 (NLT)._

I encourage you to surrender your life _(body, soul, heart and mind)_ to Jesus Christ and His Kingdom.

".... the Kingdom of God is not a matter of what we eat or drink, but of living a life of goodness and peace and joy in the Holy Spirit" Romans 14:17 NLT).

I urge you to learn of the mysteries of God's Kingdom which you must follow in order _to be saved_ from the coming wrath of God. It is IMPERATIVE to live according to God's Spirit prior to the return of Jesus Christ. In fact, it is important to live this way more than at any other time in your life! Unfortunately, many are not obedient to the leading of the Spirit! This is because our sinful nature wants to do evil, which is just the opposite of what God's Spirit wants.

If we seek obedience, God's Spirit will give us the _desires_ of our hearts which are averse to our sinful nature. For the Holy Spirit will guide and comfort us in all truth! John spoke of this revelation when he said: "However, when He, the Spirit of truth, has come, He will guide you into all truth; for He will not speak on His own authority, but whatever He hears He will speak; and He will tell you things to come" John 16:13 (NKJV).

Because of the deception and the lust within our hearts, many believers fail to see the wickedness they are doing! We must crucify the abnormal appetite _(lusting for the things of world)_ in our lives. However, _to see_ our faults versus the things of God is very difficult! Jesus, like Isaiah, prophesied that the followers of Christ would be spiritually blind. Both Matthew and Paul reveal this truth in Scripture. "And in them the prophecy of Isaiah is fulfilled, which says: 'Hearing you will hear and shall not understand and seeing you will see and not perceive" Matthew 13:14(NKJV). This spiritual deficiency has resulted in a multitude of today's Christians being unable to discern the voice of God's Spirit and to neither see nor hear spiritually! The only way to see and hear spiritually is to surrender our wills to Jesus and to allow God's Spirit to work within us.

God is omniscient *(knows everything)*, He foreknew the weaknesses of human flesh and made a way for all of us to overcome this spiritual deficiency. He foreknew that man would fail the Garden of Eden experience and would be thrust into sin and into a bondage of corruption. "For all have sinned and fall short of the glory of God" Romans 3:23 (NKJV). While God's curse fell upon Adam and Eve in the garden, and subsequently upon the entire world; humans *who* believe in Jesus are delivered from this bondage. "For the creation was subjected to futility, not willingly, but because of Him who subjected it in hope; because the creation itself also will be delivered from the bondage of corruption into the glorious liberty of the children of God" Romans 8:20-21 (NKJV).

Because of the curse, God *subjects* His creation to vanity *(futility)*, but He also subjects it in _hope_. Vanity is whatever is devoid of truth and appropriateness, perverseness, depravity, frailty and want of vigor. Therefore, the Holy Spirit must work in our hearts *(flesh)* to transform us from a life of being vain!

Here is the revelation of Romans 8:20-21. God desires spiritual children who love, trust and obey His Word! Therefore, He created spiritual beings in the form of Adam and Eve to multiply and have dominion over the entire earth. God's process to obtain mature and faithful sons and daughters meant also allowing situations of hope, peace, hardships, despair and suffering. This process proves that those who endure and overcome the circumstances of this perverted world, while maintaining their faith in God and Jesus Christ, can obtain salvation and become His children.

Hence, the trials, tests, afflictions and tribulations we encounter were set-forth by God through Satan and his demons _for a Divine reason._ God tests the hearts, love, endurance, and faith of His people! Passing the tests results in eternal life with future glory! "Yet what we suffer now is nothing compared to the glory He will reveal to us later. For all creation is waiting eagerly for that future day when God will reveal who his children really are" Romans 8:18-19 (NLT). Remember, our hope comes in the form of Jesus' blood and the power of the Holy Spirit.

Because God loves His creation and desires to save all, He set forth His _order_ in the earth. Subsequently, He established a way of redemption, yet His order is _conditional_. God's blessings, spiritual maturity, salvation, etc. is dependent upon human choices. God gave humanity the option to be redeemed and saved through Jesus Christ and the power of His Spirit. "For God so loved the world that He gave His only begotten Son, that whoever believes in Him should not perish but have everlasting life. For God did not send His Son into the world to condemn the world, but that the world through Him might be saved" John 3:16-17(NKJV).

Those who do not love Jesus or are unable to surrender their lives to Him will remain in bondage. There are multitudes in the church that are spiritually blind who remain in bondage because they lack the knowledge needed to be redeemed. It is the followers of Christ, which include many of today's Christians that Jesus and Isaiah referred to as being blind to the ways of God. Jesus said, "Therefore I speak to them in parables, because seeing they do not see, and hearing they do not hear, nor do they understand" Matthew 13:13(NKJV). Parables are earthly stories with a heavenly meaning which is only revealed to believers with spiritual eyes and ears. In the seven letters Jesus wrote to the churches in Asia, He demonstrated this truth by saying, "He who has an ear, let him hear what the Spirit says to the churches" Revelation 2:29(NKJV).

Deliverance and salvation seems easy when we read it in the Bible or hear it being ministered; however, applying God's laws and principles in our life can be difficult! It is difficult because our sinful nature unknowingly resists a spiritual transformation. A multitude of God's people continue to lust after the things of this world. For this reason, Satan attempts to influence believers by constantly placing the cares of this world before them. He does this so Christians will seek the desires of a lustful heart and fall into sin rather than remain obedient to the cause of God's Kingdom!

If God's people, who believe in Jesus, would live according to His Spirit and totally depend upon Jesus, life would be so much better. Living according to the Holy Spirit is known as life in God's Kingdom where Jesus Christ rules and reigns. The Kingdom of God is energized by the Holy Spirit and is made available to lead and guide us in all truth and righteousness! This is the Word and the way of The Lord! We need the Holy Spirit.

CHAPTER TWO

The Absolute Necessity of the Holy Spirit!

Most Christians live their lives believing God will bless them and supply all their needs. While this is true, believers need to discern the type of blessing that Scripture refers to and is important to the Lord. An important and often quoted Scriptures illustrating God's blessing is found in Philippians.

.... "And my God shall supply all your need according to His riches in glory by Christ Jesus" Philippians 4:19 (NKJV).

The problem with some of our assessment of this Scripture is somewhat skewed. Many people think it refers to the blessing of *material things,* like the things of this world we desire. Many times, it does but the greater blessing to be obtained is our spiritual growth. The Father is concerned with the development of our love, gifts, talents, humility, spiritual and moral values and more. He is concerned with how we develop in His Spirit and how our development promotes the Kingdom of God.

As a believer, we must face reality in our walk with the Lord! The beginning point in our relationship with Jesus is to recognize that we are *sinful flesh* in need of a spiritual change. King David revealed his iniquity and sin in His prayer to the Father. He said, "Behold, I was brought forth in iniquity, and in sin my mother conceived me" Psalm 51:5(NKJV). Paul made known the truth of human flesh when he stated, "For all have sinned and fall short of the glory of God, being justified freely by His grace through the redemption that is in Christ Jesus" Romans 3:23-24 (NKJV). By believing in Christ Jesus, we acknowledge our sinful nature and seek God's redemption and restoration plan for our lives. This is a great thing! A far greater matter is to remain grounded in truth as we develop and mature in God's Word.

After the great fall, humans became sinful flesh. Paul acknowledged, "For I know that in me *(that is, in my flesh)* nothing good dwells; for to will is present with me, but how to perform what is good I do not find" Romans 7:18 (NKJV). Nevertheless, as faithful Christians, we are not expected to stay this way! Remember, the curse subjected all humans to vanity *(futility),* not willingly, but in hopes that one day our lives will be delivered from this bondage of corruption.

Faithful believers are being delivered from the stronghold of their flesh every day. It is because their hearts are right, and they seek the fullness of God's will in their lives. Hence, they know that "everything will not turn up roses" or "be a flowery bed of ease" because they experience and know the Scripture that reminds us of the tribulation we must face in life. However, God is faithful and has given us the power to endure and overcome the adversities of this world!

Our deliverance comes through Jesus Christ and through the power of the Holy Spirit. No, deliverance is not easy because the pathway to spiritual life is very challenging! Jesus said, "Enter by the narrow gate; for wide is the gate and broad is the way that leads to destruction, and there are *many* who go in by it. Because narrow is the gate and difficult is the way which leads to life, and there are _few_ who find it" Matthew 7:13-14(NKJV). Consequently, our foremost conquest in life is to develop and mature in the things of God. Those who develop and grow in the Lord and mature according to His Spirit to the image of Christ will become God's adopted children. "For as many as are led by the Spirit of God, these are sons _(children)_ of God" Romans 8:14 (NKJV).

God's Spirit Knows What to Pray!

Perhaps you may be asking yourself, how does a weak Christian overcome the adversities of this world and do God's will. To answer that question, we go directly to the works of the Holy Spirit who intercedes to God for us! God's Spirit not only knows the weakness of our sinful flesh, but He also knows God's will in our lives. Therefore, He makes a petition or intercedes to God, the Father on our behalf. Paul revealed, "Likewise the Spirit also helps in our weaknesses. For we do not know what we should pray for as we ought, but the Spirit Himself makes intercession for us with a groaning which cannot be uttered.

Now He who searches the hearts knows what the mind of the Spirit is, because He makes intercession for the saints according to the will of God. Since we don't know what God wants us to pray for, and we know that all things work together for good to those who love God, to those who are the called according to His purpose. For whom He foreknew, He also predestined to be conformed to the image of His Son, that He might be the firstborn among many brethren. Moreover, whom He predestined, these He also called; whom He called, these He also justified; and whom He justified, these He also glorified" Romans 8:26-30 New King James Version (NKJV).

God knew His people in advance and He chose them to become like his Son, so that His Son would be the firstborn among many brothers and sisters. And having chosen them, He called them to come to Him. And having called them, He gave them right standing with Himself. And having given them right standing, He gave them His glory. As stated in the above Scripture, God foreknew His creation.

Now for those whom God foreknew, He predestinated to be conformed to the image of His Son. Conforming means you are behaving in a way that you are expected to or supposed to behave. For whom He foreknew He also called. The word call is used particularly of the Divine call to partake of the blessings of redemption and to be a witness in the Kingdom of God. Those whom God calls, these He also justified. Justified means to declare and/or pronounce the believer to be just, righteous, or such as he ought to be. And finally, those whom God justified are also glorified. Glorification is to cause the dignity and worth of some person or thing to become manifest and acknowledged.

This process occurs in the fullness of God's time. Against its will, God's creation was subjected to His curse. But with eager hope, God's creation looks forward to the day when we will join in glorious freedom from death and decay. Many Christian leaders fail to understand that the purpose of God's creation is to call, develop and mature adopted children for His service. "Even before he made the world, God loved us and chose us in Christ to be holy and without fault in his eyes. God decided in advance to adopt us into his own family by bringing us to himself through Jesus Christ. This is what he wanted to do, and it gave him great pleasure" Ephesians 1:4-5(NLT). The works of God's Spirit, in addition to His intercessions, are designed to bring these things about!

Because Jesus only spent a limited time on the earth, God sent the Holy Spirit to dwell in human flesh and to provide a spiritual metamorphosis *(transformation in godly knowledge, wisdom and deed)* within the hearts of faithful believers. The Spirit comes to guide, teach and mature believers according to God's will. "And it shall come to pass in the last days, said God; I will pour out of my Spirit upon all flesh: and your sons and your daughters shall prophesy, and your young men shall see visions, and your old men shall dream dreams" Acts 2:17 (KJV).

The Holy Spirit dwells in the heart of those who believe in Jesus, and He teaches them the things that Jesus said and did *(His teachings, acts and deeds)*. "Howbeit when he, the Spirit of truth, is come, he will guide you into all truth: for he shall not speak of himself; but whatsoever he shall hear, that shall he speak: and he will shew you things to come. He shall glorify me: for he shall receive of mine, and shall shew it unto you" John 16:13-14 (KJV).

Through constant reminder of the things Jesus said and did, the Spirit can mature faithful Christians in the righteousness of God. He also helps us to maintain a disciplined life style that produces the fruits of God's Spirit. "But the fruit of the Spirit is love, joy, peace, longsuffering, kindness, goodness, faithfulness, gentleness, self-control. Against such there is no law. And those who are Christ's have crucified the flesh with its passions and desires. If we live in the Spirit, let us also walk in the Spirit. Let us not become conceited, provoking one another, envying one another" Galatians 5:22-26 (NKJV)

The Holy Spirit is an unseen power that resides in the hearts of those who love, trusts and obey God. These individuals believe in Jesus Christ as their Lord and Savior. Once a believer becomes a citizen of the Kingdom of God, both Jesus and the Holy Spirit begins to develop and mature them in the Gospel (*the good news*). The Kingdom enters the believer's heart and is demonstrated in his or her life as the individual <u>seeks</u> maturity. Each believer should pursue the maturity level that satisfies God. We know that humankind's original failure occurred in the Garden of Eden, but the process of redemption occurs in our lives somewhere between our birth and death. It happens when we seek Jesus Christ and citizenship in His Kingdom. Remember Jesus words, "But seek first the kingdom of God and His righteousness, and all these things shall be added to you" Matthew 6:33(NKJV). Those things which Jesus reference as being added to you are 1) entry into His Kingdom and 2) the spiritual attributes which produces God's righteousness.

True conversion will generate a significant and observable transformation in the life of a Christian. This is because spiritual conversion radically alters the direction and purpose of the believer's life. In time, faithful believers become living sacrifices, holy and acceptable to God. As Paul mentioned, "I beseech you therefore, brethren, by the mercies of God, that you present your bodies a living sacrifice, holy, acceptable to God, which is your reasonable service. And do not be conformed to this world, but be transformed by the renewing of your mind, that you may prove what is that good and acceptable and perfect will of God" Romans 12:1-2 (NKJV).

It is not only a matter of going to church and claiming to be a Christian but true conversion is a complete rebirth in the ways of God. We become a faithful creature with a renewed mind that hungers and thirsts for God, and the joy, peace and righteousness of His Kingdom! Unfortunately, a large percentage of individuals: Never spiritually develop, or mature past attending Sunday worship, being baptized and having their names on the role of a church.

We see a plethora of Christians straddling the fence between the Kingdom of God and this perverted world we live in! Hopefully in time, these individuals will experience true conversion as they hear more of the Word of God. Thankfully there are some faithful believers who seek God's Kingdom for what it is and surrender their all to the power of God's Spirit. These individuals learn how to put to death the lust and desires of their flesh which stands in opposition to obedience to God's Word.

Every Christian is probably aware of his or her secret desires for the things of this world and should be aware of how these desires interfere with Christian development. Please understand that our flesh is the sinful nature of man, with its cravings that incite us to sin. Human flesh is our earthly nature. At birth, it separated us from divine influence and made us therefore prone to sin and opposition to God. That is…until we became saved. "Because the carnal mind is enmity against God; for it is not subject to the law of God, nor indeed can be. So then, those who are in the flesh cannot please God" Romans 8:7-8 (NKJV).

A constant spiritual battle occurs daily within our hearts and minds. This confrontation is the Spirit of God battling against the lust and desires of our flesh to prevent us from doing wicked things in this world. The Holy Spirit battles the flesh of humans to influence the believers to serve the Godhead throughout their lives. As made known by the apostle Paul, "I say then: Walk in the Spirit, and you shall not fulfill the lust of the flesh. For the flesh lusts against the Spirit and the Spirit against the flesh; and these are contrary to one another, so that you do not do the things that you wish" Galatians 5:16-17(NKJV). In this scriptural text, the word _walk_ means to _regulate one's life_. To regulate one's life is to bring the flesh into conformity to the will of Jesus Christ under the rule and reign of His Kingdom. Winning this battle determines one's salvation!

Understanding what happened in the Garden of Eden is a key to understanding God's order in this world. Humans lost God's Spirit when Adam and Eve sinned by eating the fruit from the forbidden tree. Prior to Adam's and Eve's sin, God fellowshipped with them daily in the garden. However, the sin of disobedience caused spiritual _death_ and a separation from the Father. "And the LORD God commanded the man, saying, "Of every tree of the garden you may freely eat; but of the tree of the knowledge of good and evil you shall not eat, for in the day that you eat of it you shall _surely die_" Genesis 2:16-17 (NKJV). Thus, the death sentence was God detaching Himself from humans. It meant that God separated Himself from humans and no longer to personally leading and guiding them except for those whom He anointed in specific situations for His Divine purposes. Of course, all of that changed with the death and resurrection of Jesus Christ and the indwelling of the Holy Spirit.

Without God's Spirit to direct, humanity lacked spiritual guidance, discernment and had difficulty being delivered from the bondage of corruption. Human life remained this way until God gave us Jesus and poured out His Spirit on those who believe in Him. With the advent of Jesus Christ and the Holy Spirit, converted humans can now be spiritually guided. However, even with the indwelling power of God's Spirit, many still become _spiritually blind_ because of the deeds their flesh practice. These individuals are influenced by Satan to partake of the wickedness of this world while their sinful practices quench the Holy Spirit. Many live their lives enjoying the appetites of the flesh rather than becoming a living sacrifice to God. "So then, those who are in the flesh cannot please God" Romans 8:8 (NKJV).

The Bible revealed that centuries would pass before God decided to return His Spirit to humans. Without God's Spirit, Satan would run havoc over the earth. This occurs because the source of God's truth is missing in the lives of many! Even today with the indwelling of the Holy Spirit, multitudes quench the Spirit by allowing temptations to enter their hearts and to be influenced by them! "Temptation comes from our own desires, which entice us and drag us away. These desires can give birth to sinful actions. And when sin is allowed to grow *(full-grown)*, it gives birth to death [*separation from God*]" James 1:14-15(NLT). As Christians, we have the ability through God's Spirit to resist the enemy. "Therefore, submit to God. Resist the devil and he will flee from you" James 4:7(NKJV).

Regrettably, many allow the lust of their flesh to desire an object, a feeling or other type expressions that violate God's laws. Hear and understand Paul's words, "When you follow the desires of your sinful nature, the results are very clear: sexual immorality, impurity, lustful pleasures, idolatry, sorcery, hostility, quarreling, jealousy, outbursts of anger, selfish ambition, dissension, division, envy, drunkenness, wild parties, and other sins like these. Let me tell you again as I have said before, anyone living this kind of life _will not_ inherit the Kingdom of God" Galatians 5:19-21(NLT). It does not have to be this way because you have the Holy Spirit known as the Comforter!

These things cause many to stumble and fall short of deliverance from bondage! Some believers allow these expressions to grow in their hearts which eventually causes hardship in the believer's life. When the opportunity arises to express and/or indulge in these wicked acts, the flesh becomes too weak to suppress the person's desire. Only the power of God's Spirit can enable the believer to suppress these appetites and overcome the wiles of Satan. The word *wile* mean to lure, trick, scheme, entice, etc.

In many cases, a person's appetite is in opposition to God's laws. Sooner or later Satan will position that very same appetite *(adultery, fornication, idolatry, hatred, jealousy, outbursts of wrath, selfishness, murder, etc.)* before the individual and cause him or her to decide to either honor God's Word or fall into sin! As indicated before, we can resist the devil. God's Spirit gives the believer the power to resist his influences. Without the power of the Holy Spirit, humans not only struggle in day-to-day life, but they will continue to *practice* the works of the flesh.

Whenever believers surrender their will to Jesus Christ *(done through honor, prayer and supplication)* and to the power of the Holy Spirit, they can _crucify_ their flesh and resist the offerings of demonic forces. Metaphorically, the word _crucify_ is putting off the flesh with its passions and lusts. Consequently, those who are in Christ Jesus can resist theses temptations with the help of God's Spirit. I am sure you see how essential the Holy Spirit is in helping us to control our sinful nature *(our flesh)*. He works in our hearts. It is through God's Spirit that we can guard our hearts. We guard our hearts by filtering our emotions, desires, thoughts, and responses through God's Word. Whenever an unsavory emotion rises in an individual, God's Spirit begins to gently counsel the believer to realize the dangers of the act and how the act can lead to suffering and spiritual death.

Eve had the opportunity to resist the serpent, but her desire for the fruit on the forbidden tree was just too great! "So, when the woman saw that the tree was *good for food*, that it was *pleasant to the eyes*, and a tree *desirable to make one wise*, she took of its fruit and ate. She also gave to her husband with her, and he ate" Genesis 3:6 (NKJV). As Christians who hunger and thirst after righteousness, we must reframe from allowing our flesh to dictate our actions! "And those who are Christ's have crucified the flesh with its passions and desires" Galatians 5:24 (NKJV).

The anointing of God's Spirit does not manifest itself haphazardly in the believer. It is manifested when the individual believes in Jesus and seeks the will of God in his or her life. The Spirit helps believers to learn and understand the Word of God as they develop and grow. The spiritual growth occurs as believers study the Bible to show themselves approved of God. As Christians mature, God's Spirit helps us to better control our fleshly desires, so we no longer follow its nature. "He did this so that the just requirement of the law would be fully satisfied for us, who no longer follow our sinful nature but instead follow the Spirit" Romans 8:4-5 (NLT).

I am so thankful to God that He gave us the anointing power of His Spirit. Without the Spirit, the believer is unable to discern truth from mixture *(some truth mixed with false teachings)* "These things we also speak, not in words which man's wisdom teaches but which the Holy Spirit teaches, comparing spiritual things with spiritual. But the natural man does not receive the things of the Spirit of God, for they are foolishness to him; nor can he know them, because they are spiritually discerned" 1 Corinthians 2:13-14 (NKJV).

Seek to Know the Holy Spirit!

While most Christians know about the Holy Spirit, many are unaware of His origin and why He was made available to us by God. The revelation of His beginning will surprise most Christians, because few realize how God ordained the order of this world before it was even made! God chose us to be in Jesus Christ before the world was made. The same is true with every spiritual blessing God gave us which includes the Holy Spirit. Paul, an apostle of Jesus Christ, who was spiritually taught by Jesus Christ revealed this amazing truth. God knowing all things made the promise of Jesus Christ and the Holy Spirit before the world existed.

Jesus was foreordained before the world was made! "He *(Jesus)* indeed was foreordained before the foundation of the world, but was manifest in these last times for you" 1 Peter 1:20(NKJV). God made this promise to those who would be believe in Jesus Christ and would become faithful. "For God so loved the world that He gave His only begotten Son, that whoever believes in Him should not perish but have everlasting life" John 3:16 (NKJV). Additionally, God blessed us with every spiritual blessing in the heavenly places in Christ. With this revelation, we can easily see God's power in the universe. Hence, God's promises have the power and ability to transform sinful flesh into believers who would become holy and without blame. See Paul's revelation below:

> *"Blessed be the God and Father of our Lord Jesus Christ, who has blessed us with* every spiritual blessing *in the heavenly places in Christ, just as He chose us in Him before the foundation of the world, that we should be holy and without blame before Him in love, having predestined us to adoption as sons by Jesus Christ to Himself, according to the good pleasure of His will, to the praise of the glory of His grace, by which He made us accepted in the Beloved" Ephesians 1:3-6 (NKJV).*

Scripture also records God's prophecy of the Spirit. "And it shall come to pass in the last days, says God, that I will pour out of My Spirit on all flesh; your sons and your daughters shall prophesy, your young men shall see visions, your old men shall dream dreams" Acts 2:17 (NKJV). Jesus acknowledged this promise to His apostles. "Behold, I send the Promise of My Father upon you; but tarry in the city of Jerusalem until you are endued with power from on high" Luke 24:49(NKJV). We seek the fullness of this power by seeking God's Kingdom and His righteousness.

As Christians mature in the things of God, they begin to recognize the subtle but gentle voice of the Holy Spirit. Many times, at that moment before saying something derogatory or engaging in a sinful act, God's Spirit will caution the believer on the hurt such behavior would cause and offer a godly alternative. When this type interaction occurs, it is like basking in the presence of God. The Spirit is so gentle; yet He can be very effective if we allow Him to be! We learn this in Jesus' teachings of the Gospel where He directs our steps! When you realize what has happen in these situations, you become very thankful to God for His Son and His Spirit. King David spoke of the heritage of the righteous when he said, "The steps of a good man are ordered by the lord; and He is delighted in his way" Psalm 37:23 (KJV).

The Holy Spirit is the Guarantee of Our Inheritance!

Once sealed *(joining two things together)* by the Spirit, our salvation is conditionally promised until the Day of Judgment. "In Him you also trusted, after you heard the word of truth, the gospel of your salvation; in whom also, having believed, you were sealed with the Holy Spirit of promise, who is the guarantee of our inheritance until the *redemption* of the purchased possession, to the praise of His glory" Ephesians 1:13-14 (NKJV). Redemption is the act of being saved from sin, error or evil.

The inheritance is the eternal blessedness of the Kingdom of God which will become visible upon the return of Jesus Christ. In other words, the sealing of God's Spirit guarantees salvation to faithful and obedient believers. This guarantee is based upon our faithfulness, obedient to God's Word and living according to the guidance of the Holy Spirit. Consequently, without the _active_ indwelling power of God's Spirit in Christians, there is no salvation. Therefore, Christians must live their lives without quenching the Spirit through our sins. Not only that, "Dear friends, if we deliberately continue sinning after we have received knowledge of the truth, there is no longer any _sacrifice_ that will cover _these sins_" Hebrews 10:26(NLT).

As indicated before, this guarantee is conditional just like salvation is to those who believe in Jesus Christ. "That whoever _believes in Him_ should not perish but have eternal life. For God so loved the world that He gave His only begotten Son, that whoever believes in Him should not perish but have everlasting life. For God did not send His Son into the world to condemn the world, but that the world through Him might be saved" John 3:15-17(NKJV). The promise is that those who believe in Jesus will not perish but have eternal life: The key to fulfillment is the belief of Christians. If you believe and live by the Holy Spirit, you will be saved!

God set spiritual conditions for salvation. "Therefore, brethren, we are debtors—not to the flesh, to live according to the flesh. For if you live according to the flesh _you will die_; but if by the Spirit you put to death the deeds of the body, _you will live_" Romans 8:12-13 (NKJV). Perhaps the spiritual conditions set by God are new to you, but eternal salvation only comes to believers who live according to God's Spirit!

Jesus prophesied and illustrated this truth in several parables. Later, you will read of this truth being illustrated in the parable of the wise and foolish virgins. God enables believers to regulate their lives according to the leading and guiding of His Spirit. This scenario is also known as life in the Kingdom of God. As God's Spirit delivers us from the bondage of our flesh, He also instills love, peace, joy and happiness in our hearts.

The Holy Spirit is the *multiplied* source of our knowledge, understanding, strength, comfort and deliverance from the enemy. God's power *(the Holy Spirit)* from on high is the subsequent power source apart from Jesus that enables faithful believers to resist Satan and His demonic forces. Resistance is the key to receiving salvation! When a believer is obedient to God's Word, it explains the unique metamorphosis which occurs in the character, personality, temperament, spirit, attitude, and deeds of that Christian. Once an individual believes in Jesus as His/her Lord and Savior, he or she is sealed with the Holy Spirit of promise who is the guarantor of our redemption. The moment a believer receives the Holy Spirit is the moment they *first believe*.

As mentioned before, when you believe in Jesus Christ, God identifies you as His own by giving you the Holy Spirit. Your body becomes the temple of the Holy Spirit. "Or do you not know that your body is the temple of the Holy Spirit who is in you, whom you have from God, and you are not your own? For you were bought at a price; therefore, glorify God in your body and in your spirit, which are God's" 1 Corinthians 6:19-20 (NKJV).

The believer is indwelled with God's Spirit until the Day of Redemption. The Holy Spirit remains *active* in the believer unless he/she quenches *(to put out a fire, flame, i.e. extinguish)* the Spirit. Quenching of the Spirit occurs because of the believer's lustful desires. Consequently, quenching God's Spirit is metaphorically like putting out a roaring fire. The Spirit becomes dormant and no longer assists the Christian in the things of God. He remains indwelled in the believer, but because He is quenched, the Spirit is not active or growing or being used at that particular time in life. The Holy Spirit is capable of becoming active later in the believer's life if the believer repents of their sin with a contrite heart, ask the Lord for forgiveness, turn away from their sins and ask to be refilled with the Holy Spirit of God.

As the third person of the Trinity, the Holy Spirit is fully God. God's Spirit is eternal, omniscient *(all knowing)*, and omnipresent *(everywhere at the same time)* has a will, and can speak. He is alive and powerful! The Bible declares that the Holy Spirit is the power of God on earth and He leads believers into all truth. He also enables the believer to discern spiritual truths. In addition, He is our guarantee of eternal life in the resurrection when we obey God's laws and principles. Without the Spirit in our lives, we cannot belong to God. "But you are not in the flesh but in the Spirit, if indeed the Spirit of God dwells in you. Now if anyone does not have the Spirit of Christ, he is not His" Romans 8:9 (NKJV). Many profess and even brag about belonging to Jesus yet, if the Holy Spirit is not *active within the heart* of the believer, he or she does not belong to Jesus.

Being indwelled by the Holy Spirit makes the believer a unique and special individual before God. As Christian believers, we must crucify our flesh of sexual sins because we have become the temple of God's Spirit. "Run away from all sin… especially from sexual sin! No other sin affects the body as clearly as this one does. For sexual immorality is a sin against your own body. "Don't you realize that your body is the *temple of the Holy Spirit*, who lives in you and was given to you by God? You do not belong to yourself, for God bought you with a high price. So you must honor God with your body" 1 Corinthians 6:18-20 (NLT). Did you know that once you become Spirit-filled, you do not belong to yourself, we belong to God? Therefore, belonging to God means we must hear His voice and do as He says!

Simply speaking, the Holy Spirit is _God living in us!_ Please do not forget that! The Holy Spirit is equal with the Father and the Son, Jesus Christ. He is present in the hearts of believers to make them aware of their need for Jesus Christ and to be governed by His Words. I see many ministers illustrating the _works_ of Jesus, what He did, rather than _His teachings_. It is in Jesus' teachings where truth prevails, and we find instructions on how to live as Christians.

The acts of Jesus are important, but it is in His teachings that we learn _how to live_ according to God's Word. Once we concentrate on His teachings, the Holy Spirit is there to give us the revelation of the mysteries He taught. The Spirit then provides faithful believers with the power for living, the understanding of spiritual truths, and guidance in doing what is right. As Christians, we should seek to live according to God's Spirit's and enjoy the benefits He provides through His anointing. Listed below are some of the major benefits of the Holy Spirit:

- _God's Spirit begins a work in us which, in time, transforms us into the image of Christ._
- _The Holy Spirit gives power. "But you shall receive power when the Holy Spirit has come upon you; and you shall be witnesses to Me in Jerusalem, and all of Judea and Samaria, and to the end of the earth" Acts 1:8._
- _The Holy Spirit leads us and empowers us in the maturing and development process. He helps us to learn obedience to the Word of God in our sufferings and to be led into perfection, just as Jesus was._
- _The power of the Holy Spirit strengthens us to endure so that we do not lose heart and enables us to stand firm until the end!_
- _The Holy Spirit is a Helper. The Helper guides us into all the truth, convicting us of sin, of righteousness, and judgement._

- *If we walk (regulate our lives) in the Spirit, we will not fulfill the lusts of the flesh.*
- *The Holy Spirit is our intercessor. "Likewise the Spirit also helps in our weaknesses. For we do not know what we should pray for as we ought, but the Spirit Himself makes intercession for us with groaning's which cannot be uttered" Romans 8:26 (NKJV).*
- *The Spirit is a conduit of gifts. Jesus gave diversities of gifts to His disciples through the Holy Spirit: gifts such as of healing, prophecy, tongues and interpretation, the Word of knowledge, the Word of wisdom, working of miracles, discerning of spirits, etc.*
- *The Holy Spirit comforts the believer. "Then the churches throughout all Judea, Galilee, and Samaria had peace and were edified. And walking in the fear of the Lord and in the comfort of the Holy Spirit, they were multiplied" Acts 9:31 (NKJV).*

Expectations of God through His Spirit!

God expects a spiritual transformation to occur in those who believe in Jesus and live their best lives according to His Spirit. Many changes occur in humans for the better as the result of God's indwelling Spirit. _Bearing the fruit of the Spirit_ is one of the most important! Bearing the fruit of God's Spirit demonstrates the likeness of Christ. Not all believers bear fruit as called by God to do! Yet, many profess to be born-again, baptized in water and filled with the Holy Spirit. Unfortunately, a multitude of Christians who profess Christianity have experienced very little change in their behavior and character. These Christians grieve the Spirit without repentance or quench the Spirit… which ultimately leads to spiritual death!

Being filled with God's Spirit is no small matter. In fact, it is a thing of wonder and amazement! Being filled with the Spirit produces the gifts of the Spirit when the believer is submitted to Jesus Christ as

Lord and Savior. Scripture reads, "But the Holy Spirit produces this kind of fruit in our lives: love, joy, peace, patience, kindness, goodness, faithfulness, gentleness, and self-control. There is no law against these things! Those who belong to Christ Jesus have nailed the passions and desires of their sinful nature to his cross and crucified them there. Since we are living by the Spirit, let us follow the Spirit's leading in every part of our lives. Let us not become conceited, or provoke one another, or be jealous of one another" Galatians 5:22-26 (NLT). The manifestation of these fruits of the Spirit in the mature believer demonstrates citizenship in the Kingdom of God.

Please understand that being born-again means that those who are born of God *do not* sin, for God's *seed* remains in them; and they cannot sin, because these individuals have been born of God. God's *seed* is the Divine energy of the Holy Spirit operating in the soul of a person by which we are regenerated. However, "Dear children, don't let anyone deceive you about this: When people do what is right, it shows that they are righteous, even as Christ is righteous. But when people keep on sinning, it shows that they belong to the devil, who has been sinning since the beginning. But the Son of God came to destroy the works of the devil. Those who have been born into God's family do not make a practice of sinning, because God's life is in them. So they can't keep on sinning, because they are children of God" 1 John 3:7-9 (NLT).

In God's Kingdom, faithful believers are transformed into matured saints of God. The opposite applies as well. If believers are not faithful when they seek God's Kingdom and His righteousness, they do not mature into saints of God! They remain as believers seeking God's will in their lives. As saints, the believers become God's adopted sons and daughters! This occurs because God imparts a measure of

Himself in human flesh and the believers live obediently to God's causes and promotes His Kingdom.

One of the joys of Christianity is seeing the Holy Spirit bring about spiritual and physical growth in a believer. The measure of God in us produces love, faith, forgiveness, grace and understanding. Subsequently, the believer becomes a light to the entire world to see! "You are the light of the world. A city that is set on a hill cannot be hidden. Nor do they light a lamp and put it under a basket, but on a lampstand, and it gives light to all who are in the house. Let your light so shine before men, that they may see your good works and glorify your Father in heaven" Matthew 5:14-16 (NKJV).

The Bible identifies numerous reports of God's Spirit empowering human flesh to perform a godly mission. The Spirit helps humans to rise above their carnal minds and sinful nature to perform extraordinary tasks in God's Kingdom. These saints are acknowledged as holy and/or virtuous beings bound for heaven. Exhibiting the fruits of God's Spirit demonstrates that the believer has indeed matured in the ways of Jesus Christ. Being filled with the Spirit means a believer has become the righteous temple of the Holy Spirit unless the individual quenches the Spirit.

Remember, individuals quench God's Spirit by surrendering their heart to the lust of worldly entities. Paul reveals the origin of the temple of the Holy Spirit. "Don't you realize that your body is the temple of the Holy Spirit, who lives in you and was given to you by God? You do not belong to yourself, for God bought you with a high price. So you must honor God with your body" 1 Corinthians 6:19-20(NLT). In other words, the temple of the Holy Spirit is God's sanctuary *(a holy place)* where a measure of Him resides in the hearts of faithful believers. We are not our own for we belong to God and therefore, we must constantly *glorify* God in our bodies *(by the things we do)* and in our spirit, which belongs to Him.

Glorify means to worship, honor, praise, magnify, revere, sanctify, bless, and adore God with all of our heart, mind, soul and spirit! "Now may the God of patience and comfort grant you to be like-minded toward one another, according to Christ Jesus, that you may with one mind and one mouth *glorify* the God and Father of our Lord Jesus Christ" Romans 15:5-6 (NKJV). This we shall do because it is part of the redemption process.

God has given us a way of redemption through His Spirit; He enables us to become righteous beings before His throne. The apostle Paul exclaimed, "For what the law could not do in that it was weak through the flesh, God did by sending His own Son in the likeness of sinful flesh, on account of sin: He condemned sin in the flesh, that the righteous requirement of the law might be fulfilled in us who do not walk according to the flesh but according to the Spirit" Romans 8:3-4(NKJV).

CHAPTER THREE

You Can Put the Fire Out!

Ever since the world was created, there has been a consistent
deficiency *(something the body needs)* among the majority of God's
people. This deficiency is the *inability* to judge our own hearts relative
to God's will and His Word. We saw this same capacity occur with
Eve in the Garden of Eden and later in the Old Testament with Jonah.
Both individuals reaped God's judgment and penalty for not obeying
His commandments.

Most Christians are aware of Eve's failure in eating the forbidden fruit
which caused humankind to be disciplined with a curse. Many of us
look at Adam and Eve's situation as an interesting story or fable but
fail to understand the judgments of God when they do not judge
ourselves. "For if we would judge ourselves, we would not be judged.
But when we are judged, we are chastened by the Lord, that we may
not be condemned with the world" 1 Corinthians 11:31-32 (NKJV).

In Jonah's case, God told him to go to Nineveh. Instead of obeying
God, Jonah arose and fled to Tarshish from the presence of the LORD.
Then the LORD sent out a mighty tempest on the sea, so that the ship
was about to be broken up. Because the mariners were afraid, they
threw Jonah overboard to lighten the load on the ship and the men
also thought the storm came because Jonah was on the ship.
Subsequently, when Jonah was tossed from the ship, the Lord had
arranged for a great fish to swallow him. Jonah was inside the fish for

three days and three nights. After Jonah prayed to God, the LORD ordered the fish to spit Jonah out onto the beach. Then the LORD spoke to Jonah a second time about going to Nineveh and he repented and then obeyed the LORD's command and traveled on to Nineveh. Judgment comes to us when we disobey God's commandments and His will. However, He is the God of second chances. Many believers have been given second chances and more, including me.

Even in today's church, God's people often have a difficult time *examining* their own hearts in relationship to honoring God's Word. As Paul revealed, "Examine yourselves to see if your faith is genuine. Test yourselves. Surely you know that Jesus Christ is among you; if not, you have failed the test of genuine faith" 2 Corinthians 13:5(NLT). Many in the body of Christ practice iniquity without knowing the merits of their own character and hearts. This happens because multitudes have not sought to know God's Word or the essence of His Kingdom to do the comparisons. Failure to seek God's Kingdom and His righteousness means the believer simply never sought or been taught the truth nor how to procced into a life in the Kingdom!

Sufficient to say, one day each one of us will have to give an account to Jesus Christ. "So then each of us shall give account of himself to God" Romans 14:12 (NKJV). Our testimony will be the quintessential account *(a solemn declaration)* that all of God's people will have to surrender to Jesus. This account will be the essence of how we lived our lives on earth. Our testimony will determine our eternal destiny. At Judgment time, we will obtain Jesus' assessment of our lives and the truth regarding God's Divine order for this world.

Many words have been ministered by church leaders regarding how we shall live and whether God's grace will apply to our final judgment. For many, God's judgment will be quite severe because of the individual's life account, while others receive eternal life. The Bible gives ample direction to God's people so we do not have to live out a lifetime to find-out our plight *(a condition or state of affairs)* in life at the last day! We can discover our destiny simply by studying the Word of God for ourselves.

Jesus tells us to work hard to enter the narrow gate to God's Kingdom, for many will try to enter but will fail because of the iniquity they practiced. I repeat this statement many times over in my writings because I see so many Christians ignoring the fact that our flesh is *really* one of our greatest enemies. Those who practice the works of their flesh will not inherit the Kingdom of God *(Galatians 5)*. However, those who are in Christ and are Kingdom citizens have crucified their flesh with its passions and desires. Hopefully you know who you are and what is in your heart because Jesus' judgments will be true! Unlike humans, He will look upon the heart of man. Throughout God's Word *(the Bible)* we see His judgments occur many times over… relative to how a person lived his or her life. Therefore, we won't be surprised about our own verdict on Judgment Day!

We saw the first expression of God's judgment before the world was formed when He judged the king of Tyre *(Satan)*. He said, "You were perfect in your ways from the day you were created, till iniquity was found in you" Ezekiel 28:15 (NKJV). Iniquity is the unrighteousness in one's heart and life. It's the manifestation of lawlessness and/or wickedness in our being. It is a flesh condition of not being right with God, according to the standard of His holiness.

We see another form of judgment in Jesus' prophecy of ministers who allowed their flesh to direct their lives. "Not everyone that says unto me, Lord, Lord, shall enter into the kingdom of heaven; but he that does the will of my Father which is in heaven. Many will say to me in that day, Lord, Lord, have we not prophesied in thy name? And in thy name have cast out devils? And in thy name done many wonderful works? And then will I profess unto them, _I never knew you_: depart from me, ye that work iniquity" Matthew 7:21-23 (KJV). Jesus Christ pronounced that He does not know those who continually commit iniquity. Let this be a warning to all believers who's Christianity revolves from hot to cold.

A similar prophecy came when one of Jesus followers asks Him about the salvation of God's people. He responded in kind, "When one said to Him, "Lord, are there few who are saved?" And He said to them, "Strive to enter through the narrow gate, for many, I say to you, will seek to enter and will not be able. When once the Master of the house has risen up and shut the door, and you begin to stand outside and knock at the door, saying, 'Lord, Lord, open for us,' and He will answer and say to you, 'I do not know you, where you are from,' then you will begin to say, 'We ate and drank in Your presence, and You taught in our streets.' But He will say, 'I tell you _I do not know you_, where you are from. Depart from Me, all you workers of iniquity" Luke 13:22-27 (NKJV). This is a direct message to those who go through the motions of Christianity but fail to become faithful believers who love God with all their heart, mind and soul.

Faithful Believers Walk According to the Spirit!

Now is the time for believers to re-examine their own character and evaluate how it relates to the work of the Holy Spirit! As an example, do you have some deep secret in your heart that grieves the Spirit or are you involved in ungodly behavior such as adultery, fornication, hatred or idolatry? It could be some generational sin that is accepted in your family. I say this because so many Christians misunderstand the fullness of God's _order_ on the earth and how it relates to righteousness.

Human flesh _can_ become righteous before God through a life surrendered to Jesus that is regulated by the Holy Spirit. _This is the only way!_ Scripture bears witness to this truth. "For what the law could not do in that it was weak through the flesh, God did by sending His own Son in the likeness of sinful flesh, on account of sin: He condemned sin in the flesh, that the righteous requirement of the law might be fulfilled in us who do not walk according to the flesh but according to the Spirit" Romans 8:3-4 (NKJV).

My friends do not be deceived! Many Christians speak of the Holy Spirit in accordance to the perceived power He gives us. Additionally, a multitude of Christians believe that the Spirit gives them the ability to bind and loose Satan, as well as rebuking demons in times of crisis. Right now, I do not want to debate this issue but rather share with you what the Spirit does in God's Kingdom.

First, let us explore again the meaning of the Kingdom of God. Paul states, "For the kingdom of God is not eating and drinking, but righteousness and peace and joy in the Holy Spirit" Romans 14:17 (NKJV). It is the royal power of Jesus as the triumphant Messiah where Jesus rules and reigns. Furthermore, the Kingdom is God is that providence that resides in the hearts of faithful believers. It is in the heart of man where God's Spirit influences believers to become righteous, resistant to the advances of Satan and fulfill his or her calling from God.

When Jesus was asked by the Pharisees about the Kingdom and when it was coming, Jesus replied and said, "The kingdom of God does not come with observation; nor will they say, 'See here!' or 'See there!' For indeed, the kingdom of God is within you" Luke 17:20-21 (NKJV). Every action first occurs in the heart of humans; both good and evil! When individuals hear the word of truth and believe in Jesus Christ as their Lord and Savior, they receive salvation and the Holy Spirit.

The apostle Paul revealed this process in Ephesians 1:13-14 (NKJV). He said, "In Him you also trusted, after you heard the word of truth, the gospel of your salvation; in whom also, having believed, you were *sealed* with the Holy Spirit of promise, who is the guarantee of our inheritance until the redemption of the purchased possession, to the praise of His glory." John stated. "Most assuredly, I say to you, he who believes in Me has everlasting life" John 6:47(NKJV).

The subsequent actions that manifest our salvation or our damnation first occur in our hearts. These states of mind include belief, faith, joy, peace and righteousness. These attributes *(quality or feature)* can be either holy and righteous or ungodly and wicked. The choice lies within the believer's heart and manifested in their character.

Just know that the Holy Spirit remains indwelled in the believer until the Day of Judgment no matter which course of life the Christian chooses! An individual may grieve the Spirit and have to repent of their sin, yet the Spirit remains in the believer. Same is true when the believer completely quenches the Spirit. The Spirit remains in the believer but is *dormant* and is no longer working on the person's behalf. If the believer grieves or quenches God's Spirit, they must humble themselves, pray, repent of their sins; stop the sinning *(turn from their wicked ways)* and ask God for forgiveness. In the case of quenching the Spirit, they must also ask the Lord to reactivate *(filling)* the Holy Spirit that is within them. The individual does not get more of the Spirit, but the Holy Spirit gets more of the individual. God's

Spirit gets more of the person's heart, mind and soul which produce more love, peace, joy and happiness in the believer. This is the maturing process of the Gospel.

Whenever a believer joins a church, they should be baptized in water, as well as, become born-again by the Holy Spirit. Jesus answered, "Most assuredly, I say to you, unless one is born of water and the Spirit, he cannot enter the kingdom of God" John 3:5(NKJV). The word _water_ is symbolically used in John 3:5 which mean a moral and practical cleansing affected by the removal of defilement when the believer _takes heed_ to the Word of God. The person is then able to live a faithful life with joy, peace and happiness. The new birth is both a spiritual and physical regeneration of your life. It produces a new and better life consecrated to God with a radically changed mind and heart.

As a citizen of God's Kingdom, the believer should experience the anointing of a transformed life. Do not look for a physical change to occur because the Holy Spirit is unseen but look to a heartfelt spiritual change where the believer's paradigm changes. His or her thoughts that were once evil are now focused on good and dependence upon God. The believer's trust in our Lord Jesus Christ grows exponentially. Hence, the believer's faith increases, and the individual depends more on Jesus for their provisions in life.

The transformation becomes their new life in God's Kingdom. Jesus says, "Therefore do not worry, saying, 'What shall we eat?' or 'What shall we drink?' or 'What shall we wear?' For after all these things the Gentiles seek. For your heavenly Father knows that you need all these things. But seek first the kingdom of God and His righteousness, and all these things shall be added to you. Therefore do not worry about tomorrow, for tomorrow will worry about its own things. Sufficient for the day is its own trouble" Matthew 6:31-34 (NKJV).

Those who experience this spiritual metamorphosis realize their lives are now filled with more love, joy, happiness, and peace beyond natural comprehension. Their worries, stress and anxieties are lessen and/or removed, because now they believe in Jesus, the promises of God and have faith that everything will be alright! As the believer grows in God's Kingdom, he or she takes on the character of Jesus by loving all of God's people. Jesus said, "But I say to you who hear: Love your enemies, do good to those who hate you, bless those who curse you, and pray for those who spitefully use you" Luke 6:27-28(NKJV). As Christians, we must seek the power of love from on high, particularly in the times in which we live. The signs of the end of the age include betrayal and hatred. However, as saints of God, we must overcome these ungodly morals and become a light to this dying generation by loving our enemies.

> *"You have heard that it was said, 'You shall love your neighbor and hate your enemy.' But I say to you, love your enemies, bless those who curse you, do good to those who hate you, and pray for those who spitefully use you and persecute you, that you may be sons of your Father in heaven; for He makes His sun rise on the evil and on the good, and sends rain on the just and on the unjust" Matthew 5:43-45 (NKJV)*

In the signs of the times, Jesus prophesied, "And then many will be offended, will betray one another, and will hate one another" Matthew 24:10(NKJV). When we display love, joy, peace and happiness in these difficult times, some *unbelievers and believers* will desire these characteristics and seek the Lord and His Kingdom for themselves. Baptism of the heart by the Holy Spirit enables Spirit-filled Christians to treat people completely different than what we normally see and hear in this perverse world. Luke quoted Jesus when He said, "Judge not, and you shall not be judged. Condemn not and you shall not be condemned. Forgive and you will be forgiven. Give and it will be given to you: good measure, pressed down, shaken together, and running over will be put into your bosom. For with the same measure that you use, it will be measured back to you" Luke 6:37-38 (NKJV).

Many *unbelievers* will seek Jesus and the godly morals of His Kingdom; when they perceive that our love, forgiveness, care and peace are genuine. Faithful believers not only have sustaining strength in Jesus, but we also have communication with the Spirit to overcome the transgressions of our flesh. Our ears become attuned to the voice of God's Spirit as He comforts, teaches and guide us into all truth. The believer learns what to do… and what not to do. They also learn how to follow the principles of God's Kingdom.

Many times, just as soon as new believers begin to mature in the things of God, tragedy strikes or some form of suffering which tests the sincerity of the individual's heart. What many ministries fail to teach new converts is to be prepared for the early phase of their new-found religion… where hardships occur most often. Many Christians attribute the tribulation to Satan's advances, which is true, but we need to look closer at the cause and effect of these sorrows. Yes, without a doubt, Satan is the culprit of this aggression because he is the ruler of this world. "The time for judging this world has come, when Satan, the ruler of this world, will be cast out" John 12:31 (NLT). Please understand this quote from the Blue Letter Bible: "Satan is under the permissive will of God, and in consequence of human sin, exercise Satanic and therefore antagonistic authority *over the world* in its present condition of spiritual darkness and alienation from God."

God allows Satan to test us for His Divine purpose. He allowed the serpent to enter the Garden of Eden to test man's heart whether they would take the alternative choice of obedience. God said humankind would encounter thorns and thistles *(trials, tests, hardships, afflictions, chastisements, hurts, pain, sufferings and more)* all the days of their life as quoted in Scripture. "Then to Adam He said, "Because you have heeded the voice of your wife, and have eaten from the tree of which I commanded you, saying, 'You shall not eat of it': "Cursed is the ground for your sake; in toil you shall eat of it all the days of your life. Both thorns and thistles it shall bring forth for you" Genesis 3:17-18 (NKJV).

Human testing is part of God's redemption plan for this world. Remember, it was the Spirit who led Jesus into the wilderness to be tested by Satan. "Then Jesus was led up by the Spirit into the wilderness to be tempted by the devil" Matthew 4:1(NKJV). It is God's will to test the hearts of His people and to prove their love, faith and endurance. This is the course of life is established develop God's adopted sons or daughters.

But shame on those who practice sin! The Apostle Paul advised the churches of Galatia that those who practice the works of their flesh fail to crucify their sinful nature. Furthermore, these individuals will not inherit the kingdom of God and are subsequently _lost_. This applies not only to unbelievers but also to Christians who allow their flesh to dominate their activities and deeds. In many of these situations, the Holy Spirit is not only grieved but is also quenched!

As temples of God's Spirit, we must live according to God's laws. As revealed before, living according to the Spirit is regulating one's life according to the ways of God by not defiling body, soul and mind.

"Do you not know that you are the temple of God and that the Spirit of God dwells in you? If anyone defiles the temple of God, God will destroy him. For the temple of God is holy, which temple you are" 1 Corinthians 3:16-17 (NKJV).

How Believers Extinguish *(Put out)* the Holy Spirit!

As a believer, are you aware that you can render the Holy Spirit inactive? I repeat, God's Spirit continues to be indwelled in all believers regardless of the circumstances of their lives, even if they _practice_ sin. The Spirit is sealed in the believer until the day of redemption. Nonetheless, the individual can quench *(extinguish)* the Spirit due to the _practice_ of ungodly deeds of their flesh. "Do not quench the Spirit" 1 Thessalonians 5:19(NKJV). As believers mature in the Holy Spirit, we must throw off our old sinful nature *(fleshly ways)* and our former way of life, which is corrupted by lust and deception. Instead, let the Spirit renew your thoughts and attitudes. Put on your new nature, created to be like God — truly righteous and holy.

Concurrent with this situation, believers can grieve the Holy Spirit with their _occasional_ sins, which is different than practicing sin. "And do not grieve the Holy Spirit of God, by whom you were sealed for the day of redemption" Ephesians 4:30 (NKJV). The Christian life is established to emulate the life of Jesus Christ. The Holy Spirit enables believers to accomplish this calling in their lives to become Christ-like. In both situations, believers must repent of their sins, ask the Lord for forgiveness, turn away from their sinful acts and ask to be filled with the Spirit again.

There are many Christians who do not know what is expected of them when they receive the Holy Spirit. Many seek the Spirit to provide materials things and give them power over demonic spirits.

There is some truth to this expression but primarily God's Spirit came to change the heart of the believer and to help him or her fulfil the commands that God called them to do! It is my hope that every believer encounters a transformation *(maturing in the Spirit)* in life as a citizen of the Kingdom of God. For the Holy Spirit is the source of our fleshly deliverance and change. Paul revealed, "Because the creation itself also will be delivered from the bondage of corruption into the glorious liberty of the children of God" Romans 8:21(NKJV). God's curse delivered His creation into bondage, but all of us can be delivered from our sinful nature through the works of Jesus Christ and the Holy Spirit. See our new nature below:

> *Therefore, putting away lying, "Let each one of you speak truth with his neighbor," for we are members of one another. "Be angry, and do not sin": do not let the sun go down on your wrath, nor give place to the devil. Let him who stole steal no longer, but rather let him labor, working with his hands what is good, that he may have something to give him who has need. Let no corrupt word proceed out of your mouth, but what is good for necessary edification, that it may impart grace to the hearers.*

> *And do not grieve the Holy Spirit of God, by whom you were sealed for the day of redemption. Let all bitterness, wrath, anger, clamor, and evil speaking be put away from you, with all malice. And be kind to one another, tenderhearted, forgiving one another, even as God in Christ forgave you" Ephesians 4:25-32 (NKJV).*

God loves us too much to leave us the way we are! Consequently, He gave us His Spirit to help believers make a spiritual transformation in life. The above Scripture describes the attributes of the saints of God who surrender their lives to Jesus Christ and are totally committed to advancing the Kingdom of God. God's kingdom is in heaven and His saints *(faithful believers of exceptional holiness)* help to bring it down to earth through the works of His Spirit. Because this endeavor is so important to believers, Jesus made it part of the Lord's Prayer. "Your kingdom come, your will be done on earth as it is in heaven" Matthew 6:10 (NKJV).

We are reminded of God's Kingdom every time we pray the Lord's Prayer. In God's Kingdom, we become righteous before Him by crucifying our flesh and living according to The Holy Spirit! Opposite of those who become saints are those who practice the works of their flesh. As stated above, *practicing* the works of your flesh can veto your salvation.

Remember, I am not talking about occasional sins which grieve the Spirit but do not quench it. I am referring to unrighteous acts of which many Christians have made a practice. I am speaking of those acts which are demonic in nature and have individuals bound in life? The word practice means doing something *regularly.* In other words, practice is an endeavor that becomes a habit or something that is repeated many times over. The ungodly works of our flesh, when continuously carried out, makes even believers unholy and unrighteous before the Lord.

Paul made a concerted effort to reveal this truth to us when he said, "Now the works of the flesh are evident, which are: adultery, fornication, uncleanness, lewdness, idolatry, sorcery, hatred, contentions, jealousies, outbursts of wrath, selfish ambitions, dissensions, heresies, envy, [c]murders, drunkenness, revelries, and the like; of which I tell you beforehand, just as I also told you in time past, that those who _practice_ such things will not inherit the kingdom of God" Galatians 5:19-21(NKJV). I believe there is a multitude of

Christians who do not understand that *practicing* the works of their flesh prohibits them from being saved.

Entering God's Kingdom is not an easy task. Jesus said "Because narrow is the gate and difficult is the way which leads to life, and there are few who find it" Matthew 7:14 (NKJV). Paul also revealed, "Strengthening the souls of the disciples, exhorting them to continue in the faith, and saying, "We must through *many tribulations* enter the kingdom of God" Acts 14:22 (NKJV). Even with tribulation, it is not a hard task to do, but it is one that requires dedication, true belief, and submission to the causes of God's Kingdom.

Bearing the Fruits of God's Spirit!

God sent a measure of Himself *(the Holy Spirit)* to the earth to work in the hearts of believers who seek Jesus Christ and His Kingdom. God's Spirit enables those believers to bear the fruit of His Spirit. "But the fruit of the Spirit is love, joy, peace, longsuffering, kindness, goodness, faithfulness, gentleness, self-control. Against such there is no law. And those who are Christ's have crucified the flesh with its passions and desires. If we live in the Spirit, let us also walk in the Spirit. Let us not become conceited, provoking one another, envying one another" Galatians 5:22-26(NKJV).

We know and understand that the Holy Spirit is in constant conflict with our flesh. Both entities seek to dominate the life of the believer! The flesh desires to satisfy our sinful nature while God's Spirit desires to transform the believer into a faithful temple of God. "Know you not that you are the temple of God, and that the Spirit of God dwells in you" 1 Corinthians 3:16 (KJV).

A plethora of Christians simply misunderstand the battle between their flesh and God's Spirit. Once again Paul's word reveals this phenomenon, "I say then: Walk in the Spirit, and you shall not fulfill the lust of the flesh. For the flesh lusts against the Spirit, and the Spirit against the flesh; and these are contrary to one another, so that you do not do the things that you wish" Galatians 5:16-17 (NKJV).

The King James Version states, "These are contrary the one to the other: so that *ye cannot do* the things that ye would. Our flesh, denotes our mere human nature; the earthly nature of man apart from divine influence and therefore prone to sin and opposed to God. Hence, our flesh needs to be controlled because it is determined to have control over the heart and soul, thus leading many into sin. To understand this confrontation better, let us review the plight of the wise and foolish virgins.

CHAPTER FOUR

And the Door Was Shut!

Imagine this scenario: A believer is alive at the time of Jesus' return to earth. God's servants are gathering believers who are _ready_ to receive Him at the wedding feast. However, one person, Sally, is out of oil which meant she had most likely quenched God's Spirit due to the deeds of her flesh and is left behind. Apparently, Sally had stop _living according to the Spirit_ and had begun living according to her flesh! At one time she was filled with the Holy Ghost and ministered the Word of God to others. Nevertheless, by the time she repented and asked God for forgiveness, the _door was already shut_ to the wedding feast! Soon thereafter the door was slightly opened, and the unrepentant Sally heard this resounding voice say, "Assuredly, I say to you, I do not know you!"

Wow! I cannot imagine what this would feel like, but it would have to be extremely devastating! Yet, it will happen to many fallen Christians attempting to enter the wedding feast! Scripture reveals that _it's going to happen!_ Think about the many days and times believers try to be good Christians but unfortunately, they surrender themselves to the lust and desires of their flesh by doing the unthinkable. Let's say the individual in another make-believe story is named Henry.

Henry got involved in a sexual relationship that he had not been able to break off. Additionally, he stole funds from his job for over a two-year period to support his sinful affair and the financial needs of his lover's family. It was their secret, no one else knew but his partner in crime. Prior to the affair, Henry was a great worker in the church, had regular attendance and even counseled others. At that time, he was full of God's Spirit and moved mightily in the Spirit. Yet something strange happened to Henry! He could no longer hear God's voice because he was living according to his flesh! Consequently, Henry grew ineffective, because his counsel began to flow from his own carnal mind and wicked heart rather than from God.

I realize the above story is *make-believe,* but in real life Christians quench God's Spirit all the time by allowing their flesh to dictate their choices in life. Their situations might result in a different set of circumstances but believe me, there are a plethora of cases where even believers give in to their flesh! I present this illustration to show you how Satan deceives God's people when they fail to realize the ungodly nature of their flesh. This happens because many fell to examine their true nature.

The parable of the wise and foolish virgins is most important to God's people because it reveals the works and deeds taken by many Christians in these last days. Jesus said, "Then the kingdom of heaven shall be likened to ten virgins who took their lamps and went out to meet the bridegroom" Matthew 25:1(NKJV). Figuratively speaking, virgins are a symbol of the local church in its relationship to Christ. In other words, the ten virgins were *all* Christians before the final day misfortunes occurred. Metaphorically, these individuals are representatives of a chaste person *(abstaining from sexual intercourse).* Virgins represent individuals who *are not* defiled.

The ten virgins are symbolic of the church which is covered by the blood of Jesus and therefore righteous in God's sight. They are guided by the power of the Holy Spirit, and they are recipients of God's gifts and callings. However, five of the virgins grieved God's Spirit and even quenched the Spirit because of their latter-day unrighteousness. This means their fallen condition was like someone who pours water on a roaring fire and puts it out! They subdued the Holy Spirit by their ungodly acts and wicked deeds! The believers could have repented, asked the Lord for forgiveness and been filled again with God's Spirit, if they could have overcome the desires of their flesh! Following repentance, the Holy Spirit enables believers to receive truth and seek the power of the Spirit to change their ways and lifestyles.

Revelation of the Parable of the Wise and Foolish Virgins

Understanding this parable can alter your life for the better if you follow its enlightenments. God's Word gives us truth, but many do not understand this truth because they are spiritually blind. As repeated many times, a plethora of God's people have quenched His Spirit which cause them to be spiritually blinded and unable to comprehend Scriptures. Please be aware that discerning the Scriptures requires spiritual knowledge and understanding. This knowledge and understanding is given only to those who study God's Word and live according to God's Spirit as Jesus disciples did.

"And the disciples came and said to Him, "Why do You speak to them *(Jesus' followers)* in parables?" He answered and said to them, "Because it has been given to you to know the mysteries of the kingdom of heaven, but to them *(Jesus followers)* it has not been given. For whoever has, to him more will be given, and he will have abundance; but whoever does not have, even what he has will be taken away from him. Therefore, I speak to them in parables, because seeing they do not see, and hearing they do not hear, nor do they understand" Matthew 13:10-13(NKJV). Jesus' followers were spiritually blinded; therefore, Jesus had to use a metaphor *(parables)* to communicate to them. At least, with the metaphors, they understood the concepts He was providing them.

Obtaining spiritual knowledge requires more than attending church and sitting on the pews. Jesus' followers began to understand this when He taught them in parables. The same holds true for us! Jesus' parables are a storehouse of mysteries and secrets which reveal God's will in the lives of His creation. If only Christians would seek to understand the truth of these parables, they would know how to proceed in life and obtain eternal life with God. The parable of the ten virgins reveals this truth. It is a depository of hidden truth regarding the salvation of God's people at the end of the age.

This parable reveals a hidden truth that many church leaders have yet to understand! It teaches that the kingdom of heaven shall be likened to ten virgins who took their lamps and went out to meet the bridegroom *(Jesus Christ)*. This parable is similar in meaning to the parable of the wheat and tares where the separation of ungodly believers from faithful believers will happen. Furthermore, the ungodly Christians who are separated will be cast into the furnace of fire and will not be allowed to enter the Kingdom of heaven.

In the parable of the wheat and tares, the tares represent ungodly Christians. The Lord describes these tares *(Christians)* as sons of the wicked one. They are the ones who have been influenced by the enemy to seek the things of this world and to follow their fleshly desires. Do not be surprise but some of the highest officials in the church have become tares *(the wicked ones)*.

After recognizing their plight in life, Jesus stated, "Let both *(wheat and tares)* grow together until the harvest. Then I will tell the harvesters to sort out the weeds [tares], tie them into bundles, and burn them, and to put the wheat in the barn" Matthew 13:30(NLT). In other words, let the faithful believers continue in the church with the ungodly Christians until Judgment Day.

On Judgment Day, they will be separated! Harvest time will be the final separation of faithful believers from those who have fallen short of God's righteousness. I pray you understand this analysis because it will help you to know your responsibilities as a godly Christian prior to Jesus' return.

Before the fall in the garden, God was active in the lives of Adam and Eve. They had a solemn relationship. So, shall it be in the lives of faithful believers. With the out-pouring of God's Spirit, God has returned to being active in the lives of those who believe in Jesus. This process is the indwelling of the Holy Spirit. When we contrast the spiritual life at the beginning of creation with today's spiritual life in God's Kingdom, we see great similarities. In the beginning, God commanded man not to eat *(partake)* of the fruit from the forbidden tree. Since man *did eat* of the fruit from the forbidden tree, he lost the ability of being in the presence of God and died *spiritually*.

At the end of the age, if humans partake of those things which quench the Holy Spirit, they will lose the activeness of God's Spirit. Consequently, they too will spiritually die because the Spirit in them will be dormant. This is what happened to the five *foolish virgins* who extinguished God's Spirit and had very little spiritual direction which caused them to lose the way to eternal life. As result of their actions, Jesus told the foolish virgins that *He did not know them!* Furthermore, they did not enter the wedding feast which symbolizes the last preparation prior to receiving eternal life.

"Then the kingdom of heaven shall be likened to ten virgins who took their lamps and went out to meet the bridegroom. Now five of them were wise, and five were foolish. Those who were foolish took their lamps and took no oil with them, but the wise took oil in their vessels with their lamps. But while the bridegroom was delayed, they all slumbered and slept.

"And at midnight a cry was heard: 'Behold, the bridegroom is coming; go out to meet him!' Then all those virgins arose and trimmed their lamps. And the foolish said to the wise, 'Give us some of your oil, for our lamps are going out.' But the wise answered, saying, 'No, lest there should not be enough for us and you; but go rather to those who sell, and buy for yourselves.' And while they went to buy, the bridegroom came, and those who were ready went in with him to the wedding; and the door was shut.

"Afterward the other virgins came also, saying, 'Lord, Lord, open to us!' But he answered and said, 'Assuredly, I say to you, I do not know you. "Watch therefore, for you know neither the day nor the hour in which the Son of Man is coming" Matthew 25:1-13(NKJV).

The *mystery* in the parable of the ten virgins illustrates the way many Christian believers will live at the end of the age. The parable identifies those who will attend the marriage supper of the Lamb *(pathway to eternal life)* from those who will not. It clearly emphasizes how individuals who quenched God's Spirit are denied entry into the wedding feast and _thus_ left to continue their wayward fleshly living. I supply you with this information, so you can discern the truth of the parable and transform the ways of your life, if necessary! Here are definitions of _key words_ from the parable to enhance your understanding. These definitions will enable you to comprehend the parable better and to understand its truth. Please reference these definitions as you study the parable and evaluate its final summary:

Virgins – Metaphorically, a chaste person who is morally pure in thought or conduct; decent and godly. All ten individuals, recorded in this parable, were once Holy Ghost filled. However, half of them lust after the things of this world and quench the Spirit.

Lamp - A lamp is a light. A vessel containing oil or alcohol burned through a wick for illumination. The lamp represents the "light and witness" of a believer. Matthew 5:14-15 (NKJV) - "You are the light of the world. A city that is set on a hill cannot be hidden. Nor do they light a lamp and put it under a basket, but on a lampstand, and it gives light to all who are in the house." A lamp supplied with oil is symbolic of a believer being indwelled by the Holy Spirit. Lamps hold very little oil and frequently needs replenishing. Christians often grieve or quench the Holy Spirit with their ungodly behaviors and must repent of their sins to become righteous again. Thus, they need to be replenished *(refilled)* with the Holy Spirit which is like a lamp needing oil. Virgins become righteous through the blood of Jesus and live according to God's Spirit.

Bridegroom – The bridegroom is our Lord Jesus Christ. In the New Testament, the image of the bridegroom is transferred from Jehovah to Jesus Christ.

Wise – The word wise refers to believers who are endowed with spiritual and practical wisdom from the Holy Spirit. They process spiritual insight of God's Word because they live according to the Spirit and they study God's Word.

Foolish – Those considered foolish are mortally worthless individuals. They lack a common-sense perception of the reality of things. They are considered scoundrels and unholy. At a point in time, all the virgins were wise believers who walked according to God's Spirit, but apparently the foolish quenched the Spirit through sin and did not repent prior to judgment.

Oil – As mentioned above, oil is symbolic of light and of the Holy Spirit.

Vessels – They are receptacles, a pail or reservoir. The word _vessel_ is known in Christian theology as a human being. Therefore, when the wise took oil in their vessels, it signifies that the believer's hearts were indwelled with the Holy Spirit.

Slumbered - In this parable, slumber means to be _negligent and careless_ because of the dulling of their spiritual senses _(they lived by the flesh and not by the Spirit)_. Slumber is also relative to false teachers. Metaphorically in 2 Peter 2:3, it is the destruction awaiting false teachers. 2 Peter 2:3 (NLT) – "In their greed they will make up clever lies to get hold of your money. But God condemned them long ago and their destruction will not be delayed."

Slept - Slept means to yield to sloth and sin. It is to be indifferent to one's salvation. To be indifferent is having no interest or concern.

Trimmed – Trim means to arrange and to put their lives in order. It is the state of order, arrangement, appearance or condition. The word _trimmed_ is symbolic of believers getting their lives together and preparing for the return of Jesus Christ.

Out – Metaphorically, _out_ means to quench or to suppress Divine influence.

Wedding – The marriage feast is the marriage supper of the Lamb *(Jesus)* to His bride *(faithful Christian believers)*. Revelation 19:7 (NKJV) - "Let us be glad, rejoice and give Him glory for the marriage of the Lamb has come, and His wife has made herself ready."

Door – The door of the Kingdom of heaven *(likened to a palace)* denotes the conditions which must be complied with to be received into God's Kingdom. Entrance is symbolically when Christ enters a believer's repentant heart. It also means to teach the word of the Kingdom. Teaching the Word of the Kingdom is considered *"loosening."* Holding back and not teaching the Word of God's kingdom is considered *"Binding."* As revealed by Jesus, the scribes and the Pharisees *bind* the Word of the kingdom by not teaching it nor did they enter the Kingdom themselves. "What sorrow awaits you teachers of religious law and you Pharisees. Hypocrites! For you shut the door of the Kingdom of Heaven in people's faces. You won't go in yourselves, and you don't let others enter either" Matthew 23:13(NLT).

Shut – To obstruct *(prevent)* entrance into the Kingdom of heaven.

Watch – It is to be on a spiritual alert. Metaphorically, watch means to give strict attention and to be cautious. It is to take heed lest through remission *(forgiveness or pardon of sins)* and indolence *(inactivity, laziness or lethargic)* some destructive calamity suddenly overtakes you.

The Revelation of the Ten Virgins!

The parable of the ten virgins sends a powerful message to all Christians who truly desire eternal life in the Kingdom of heaven. The message of this parable attempts to define the criterion required for salvation! It gives spiritual insight that is otherwise not seen or understood. This message should be the quintessential message rendered by all ministers in these last days. This truth provides Christians with the criteria for Godly living which is a prerequisite to salvation prior to the return of Jesus.

You have heard the words of Jesus which says, "For God so loved the world that He gave His only begotten Son, that whoever believes in Him should not perish but have everlasting life" John 3:16(NKJV). However, there is much more to the story! Jesus made two other statements that give clarity to development and growth in the Kingdom of God. The first is seeking to be taught by God's Spirit. The second is to realize that spiritual understanding of the mysteries and secrets of God only come by the anointing of the Spirit. He said, "But the Helper, the Holy Spirit, whom the Father will send in My name, He will _teach_ you all things, and _bring to your remembrance_ all things that I said to you" John 14:26 (NKJV). Additionally, Jesus stated, "I still have many things to say to you, but you cannot bear them now.

The things Jesus spoke of were the mysteries and secrets of the Kingdom of God. The revelation of these mysteries and secrets are only given to those who bear God's Spirit. God gives His Spirit to believers in the fullness of His time. Consequently, only those who possess spiritual discernment and knowledge can interpret the revelation of His mysteries and secrets. Obviously, the church needs more teaching relative to the indwelling and filling of God's Spirit, so more Christians will understand what the Spirit is saying to today's church.

Believers also need to know what causes the Spirit to be active or become dormant. They should also possess a sensitivity to God's

Spirit and be able to comprehend His voice, as well as, to have eyes to see and ears to hear what the Spirit is saying when He speaks!

There is one thing I find very puzzling in today's churches, and it is the messages that are being taught! We are in the last days and still many church leaders continue to minister on financial blessing, personal development and material fulfillment. Repeatedly their messages stress the importance of positive thinking and seeking fleshly blessings which include personal wealth and material blessings from the Lord. Many of their sermons seem to be just a conduit to increasing offerings and gifts to their ministries. Unfortunately, these messages cause Christian believers to lust after the things of the world rather than being matured in the Words of God's Kingdom.

The flesh, because of its woeful desires, is already a major problem to our spiritual development and growth! Our flesh needs to be crucified! A better way of saying this is: Our flesh needs to be _put to death_ and not allowed to lust after material substances. Jesus tells us to seek after the Kingdom of God and all the things we need, for they will be added unto us! Because we are in the last days, the message of the hour should be: "What is the spiritual preparation Christians should make prior to the return of Jesus?" The answer to that question is: Spiritually prepare yourself _(your flesh)_ for the return of Jesus Christ by subduing the flesh and living in the fullness of God's Spirit. Every minister should be preparing his or her membership to live this way, which is essential for salvation. God's truth flows from His Spirit to the mind and hearts of faithful and committed believers.

Remember Jesus words, "However, when He, the Spirit of truth, has come, He will guide you into all truth; for He will not speak on His own authority, but whatever He hears He will speak; and He will tell you things to come" John 16:12-13(NKJV). Therefore, let us seek God's Kingdom and allow God's Spirit to teach us the truth regarding the time and season in which we live, as well as, how to find joy, peace and happiness in this perverted world! "For the Kingdom of God is not a matter of what we eat or drink, but of living a life of goodness and peace and joy in the Holy Spirit" Romans 14:17(NLT).

As we know, God's Spirit indwells our lives to make known the mysteries of God's will, according to His good pleasure, which He purposed in Himself. God's Spirit, who is the guarantee of our inheritance, unlocks the mystery of those things which faithful believers must do on this earth! The revelation of the parable of the ten virgins is one of those messages where spiritual truth prevails. The parable unlocks secrets that believers must hear and follow. This truth reveals the last day occurrences concerning Christian inheritance and whether believers have done the right things to achieve eternal life.

This parable is Jesus' prophecy regarding His return and what happens during the period prior to His arrival. It involves His wedding feast and who shall be qualified to attend the event versus who will actually attend. The prophecy indicates that ten virgins *(symbolic of Christians)* took their lamps and went-out to meet the bridegroom *(Jesus)*. Lamps have a flame which is fed by oil. This description is characteristic of a Christian indwelled with the Holy Spirit. Whereas a lamp needs oil to manifest a flame, Christian believers need the Holy Spirit to manifest a spiritual light and establish themselves as a light to the world as witnesses. This is accomplished through the blood of Jesus Christ and the power of God's Spirit.

The revelation of the Jesus' prophecy for the last days follows! It references the bridegroom who is our Lord, Jesus Christ and Christians who will go to meet Him. The wise and foolish Christians are those individuals who makeup today's churches. It is sad to say but today's churches are filled with what another parable refers to as "wheat" and "tares" who are the same as the wise and foolish virgins in this one. As we know, separation of the wheat and tares occur in the final harvest as the "shut door" that separates the wise and foolish virgins.

Now all the Christians *(both wise and foolish virgins)*, took their lamps with them to meet the Lord. This expression is symbolic of Christian believers who become faithful witnesses and are a light and a witness to the world as empowered by the Holy Spirit. "You are the light of the world. A city that is set on a hill cannot be hidden. Nor do they light a lamp and put it under a basket, but on a lampstand, and it gives light to all who are in the house. Let your light so shine before men, that they may see your good works and glorify your Father in heaven" Matthew 5:14-16(NKJV). Please keep in mind that their lamps could only hold a very little oil and needed to be replenished frequently. The same is true with Christians. Many may need to be refilled with the Holy Spirit because of the occasional sins we commit. These sins bring us to repentance and the refilling *(filling)* of God's Spirit. This is how faithful believers maintain their righteousness. God's Will is expressed below:

> *"If My people who are called by My name will humble themselves, and pray and seek My face, and turn from their wicked ways, then I will hear from heaven, and will forgive their sin and heal their land. Now My eyes will be open and My ears attentive to prayer made in this place" 2 Chronicles 7:14-15 (NKJV).*

God sent His Spirit to the earth to accomplish His will in those who seek Jesus Christ and His Kingdom. The Holy Spirit fills believers for this purpose. The word "*fill*" means to be controlled. The filling does not mean that we as Christian believer gets more of the Holy Spirit, but rather, God's Spirit gets more of us! This means God's Spirit gets more of our heart, mind and soul. Thus, the life of the believer becomes more fruitful in the natural and in the Spirit! When allowed, the Holy Spirit produces fruit in the life of the believer. "But the fruit of the Spirit is love, joy, peace, longsuffering, kindness, goodness, faithfulness, gentleness, self-control. Against such there is no law" Galatians 5:22-23(NKJV). The Spirit also imparts gifts to faithful believers as ordained by God before the foundation of the world. See below the gifts which are rendered by the Holy Spirit:

> "But the manifestation of the Spirit is given to each one for the profit of all: for to one is given the word of wisdom through the Spirit, to another the word of knowledge through the same Spirit, to another faith by the same Spirit, to another gifts of healings by the same Spirit, to another the working of miracles, to another prophecy, to another discerning of spirits, to another different kinds of tongues, to another the interpretation of tongues. But one and the same Spirit works all these things, distributing to each one individually as He wills" 1 Corinthians 12:7-11(NKJV).

Hence, the Holy Spirit is doing His task in believers who allow His anointing to speak the truth of the last day events. The parable of the ten virgins reveals this truth for all to see and understand. The essence of this parable is that Christians must be Holy Ghost filled and baptized in water. These measures provide faithful believers with spiritual understanding of the final separation of the children of God and the children of Satan at the end of this age! Here lies the truth. I will repeat it again: The parable reveals that the foolish virgins took their lamps but took no oil in them. Metaphorically, this describes a believer who allows the works of their flesh to govern their choices in the life. Consequently, the Spirit is quenched because the believer practices these sins and causes the Spirit to become _passive._ The wise virgins took oil in their vessels with their lamps which meant these believers were Spirit-filled and regulated their lives according to the Spirit. The word _vessel_ is known in Christian theology as a human being. As shown above, oil is symbolic of light and of the Holy Spirit! This parable is the demonstration of faithful believers _(wise virgins),_ who had oil in their _vessels_ which is the same as Spirit-filled Christians who will be ready to receive Jesus at his return.

The message of many churches is positive, but sometimes ministers overlook repentance, the part where the believer must _turn from the sin_ and surrender to the Lord. Many times, they only speak to repentance and overlook the _sinning no more_ part. Repentance from sin is a change of heart and mind which involves two actions, a turning from sin and a turning to God. Confession itself is not enough to enable the believer to automatically walk in the Spirit. Believers _must_ become yielded instruments for God's services. This is achievable because a yielded vessel _(faithful believer)_ receives Divine power from on high. "Behold, I send the Promise of My Father upon you; but tarry in the city of Jerusalem until you are endued with power from on high" Luke 24:49(NKJV).

Regarding the matter of the woman who was caught in the act of adultery, Jesus demonstrated how we must treat sin and repentance. "And Jesus was left alone, and the woman standing in the midst. When Jesus had raised Himself up and saw only the woman, He said to her, "Woman, where are those accusers of yours? Has no one condemned you?" She said, "No one, Lord." And Jesus said to her, "Neither do I condemn you; go and sin no more" John 8:9-11(NKJV).

He told her to, "Go and sin no more!" True repentance not only includes asking for forgiveness, but it also means the believer is ready to stop their sinful acts. Scripture reveals that in the last days many Christians will yield to sloth and sin like the foolish virgins and not care about the penalty it brings in the end.

Here is a significant passage of Scripture from that parable. It is significant because we are living through that very same scenario right now in America. It reads, "But while the bridegroom was delayed, they all slumbered and slept" Matthew 25:5 (NKJV). The term, "They all slumbered and slept refers to the ten virgins" *(Christian churches everywhere)*. Both the wise virgins *(Faithful Christians)* and the foolish virgins *(Unfaithful Christians)* slumbered and slept which means the church would be silent in the period prior to Jesus' return. Is this not what we are experiencing and seeing today?

Slumber means to be negligent and careless while sleep means to yield to sloth and sin. It is to be indifferent to one's salvation. To be indifferent is having no interest or concern. In other words, the church, as portrayed by the wise and foolish virgins, has become silent in the face of all the immorality that is occurring in this world. In many circles, the church supports those who are causing this tremendous immoral grief. It is happening in our homes, in the work place and partially in congressional affairs. This parable illustrates the church's actions of this time. Unfortunately, part of this immoral equation is the ungodly behavior by ministers, as well as, that of their congregations. Many of these individuals are negligent and careless in their daily lives. Jesus prophesied that all these things would occur, and He was right!

Another significant revelation is the definition of the word trimming. "And at midnight a cry was heard: 'Behold, the bridegroom is coming; go out to meet him!' Then all those virgins arose and trimmed their lamps. Trimming means to arrange and/or to put their lives in order which is living according to the Spirit. "Therefore, dear brothers and sisters, you have no obligation to do what your sinful nature urges you to do. If you live by its dictates, you will die! But if through the power of the Spirit you put to death the deeds of your sinful nature, you will live" Romans 8:12-13 (NLT). I pray you understand the essence of this Scripture, because our time is short, and we must put our lives in order, living according to the Holy Spirit.

Our Lamps are Going Out!

Now I want you to get this: In the parable, the foolish virgins *(Christians)* said to the wise, "Give us some of your oil, for our lamps are going out." But the wise Christians answered, saying, 'No, lest there should not be enough for us and you; but go rather to those who sell and buy for yourselves" Matthew 25:8-9 (NKJV). This Scripture is perhaps the most significant component of what the parable conveys. It draws to our attention to the very thing that many Christians are doing in their walk with the Lord. First, the foolish virgins said to the wise virgins, "Give us some of your oil, for our lamps are going out." The expression, "Our lamps are going out" is a metaphor meaning to quench, suppress and to stifle Divine influence.

The work of the Holy Spirit, now that Jesus resides in heaven, is to impart Divine influence on Christians everywhere. Therefore, the Spirit battles our flesh daily. "The sinful nature wants to do evil, which is just the opposite of what the Spirit wants. And the Spirit gives us desires that are the opposite of what the sinful nature desires.

These two forces are constantly fighting each other, so you are not free to carry out your good intentions" Galatians 5:17 (NLT). As result of the foolish virgins' *(Christians)* behavior, they quenched the Holy Spirit and were no longer receiving His Divine influence. They now walked according to their flesh and not God's Spirit.

The very thing that compels humans to walk according to their flesh is their lust for wealth or at least a lot of money. This *lust* for money creates other ungodly behaviors that are associated with the lust for abundance. This is the way of the world, as posted by Satan. This is his greatest gift and the one he has permeated throughout Christendom, as well as, with individuals in professional employment, sports, arts, politics and other livelihoods. God spoke to Ezekiel regarding the evils of the prince of Tyre, who is Satan. Scripture regarding his gift is shown below:

> *"(Behold, you are wiser than Daniel! There is no secret that can be hidden from you! With your wisdom and your understanding you have gained riches for yourself and gathered gold and silver into your treasuries; By your great wisdom in <u>trade</u> you have increased <u>your riches</u>, and your heart is lifted up because of <u>your riches</u>)"* Ezekiel 28:3-5 (NKJV). *Trade is merchandising, trafficking which is the business of buying and selling things such as drugs or weapons illegally and trade which is the activity of buying, selling, or exchanging goods or services between people, firms, or countries.*

As you can see, the lust for money and wealth is the most malicious deed Satan uses to influence humankind. He does this because he is very skilled at it! It is really sad to see and understand how good Christians can work all their lives in the church yet hinder their calling by lusting for wealth or some other ungodly worldly attraction or vice that quenches God's Spirit. Such was the case in the life of the minister of the church at Ephesus. Jesus called out many of the churches in Asia because of their wayward ministry. Most churches pleased the Lord but there were some who did not fulfill their calling. The church of Ephesus had performed a lot of good deeds, but the ministry had left its first love, which is *the love of God and His Son, Jesus Christ.* Apparently, they turned their love to money, sexual relationships, greed, control, or many other vices which ruled their hearts over their love for God. Therefore, Jesus wrote the following letter to them.

> *"To the angel of the church of Ephesus write, 'These things says He who holds the seven stars in His right hand, who walks in the midst of the seven golden lampstands: "I know your works, your labor, your patience, and that you cannot bear those who are evil. And you have tested those who say they are apostles and are not, and have found them liars; and you have persevered and have patience, and have labored for My name's sake and have not become weary. Nevertheless I have this against you, that you have left your first love. Remember therefore from where you have fallen; repent and do the first works, or else I will come to you quickly and remove your lampstand from its place — unless you repent. But this you have, that you hate the deeds of the Nicolaitans, which I also hate"* Revelation 2: 1-6 (NKJV).*

Many Christians *(ministers and their congregants)* are unaware or cannot see the evils in which they are involved! They simply continue their ways until they are caught in the sin or become exposed to the church and/or the public. This same scenario continues to be prominent in the lives of many Christians today. Read the parable of the sower and the parable of the wheat and tares. These parables reveal the underlining issues which cause their wayward behavior. These behaviors can happen so easily because of a dull heart. Spiritual blindness comes as result of paralysis *(state of being unable to act or function properly)* in the believer's heart. Subsequently, the believer turns to the things which give him/her *physical pleasures*.

So, when the foolish virgin asked the wise virgins for some of their oil; they said No! You go rather to those who buy and sell for yourselves. It is because the foolish virgins had money, or they supported those who had money. Consequently, they were sent out to *buy* because this was the act to which they were accustomed. Buying and selling is representative of the things of this world. It is unfortunate that some corrupt the simple things in life. Apparently, the foolish virgins had been satisfying their own fleshly desires by seeking after the things of this world which so many others do! In some churches it is difficult to distinguish the house of God from the world's array of celebration. So many churches duplicate the world in the things they do as witnesses of the Gospel.

The parable points out the results of this transgression *(a breach of a law, etc.; sin or crime)*. "And while they went to buy, the bridegroom came, and those who were *ready (Spirit filled)* went in with him to the wedding; and the door was shut. Afterward the foolish virgins came also, saying, 'Lord, Lord, open to us!' But He answered and said, 'Assuredly, I say to you, I do not know you. "Watch therefore, for you know neither the day nor the hour in which the Son of Man is coming" Matthew 25:10-13 (NKJV). The Day of Judgment will be a very sad occurrence. This is because multitudes of Christians will discover that they quenched God's Spirit and lived according to the works of their flesh. "I tell you beforehand, just as I also told you in time past, that those who practice such things will not inherit the kingdom of God" Galatians 5:21 (NKJV).

The Enormous Power from on High!

Now is the time for all believers to re-evaluate the true nature of their hearts and to discern their deeds in this world. The road to God's Kingdom is very difficult! As believers, we must *surrender* ourselves to Jesus and make every effort to seek His Kingdom. It is in His kingdom where you find righteousness, peace and joy in the Holy Spirit. "The Kingdom of God is not eating and drinking, but righteousness and peace and joy in the Holy Spirit" Romans 14:17(NKJV).

Jesus reminded us of how difficult the way to life really is when He said, "Enter by the narrow gate; for wide is the gate and broad is the way that leads to destruction, and there are many who go in by it. Because narrow is the gate and difficult is the way which leads to life, and there are few who find it" Matthew 7:13-14(NKJV). Hence, many Christians will not be saved! However, it does not have to be this way! There is tremendous power in Jesus Christ and the Holy Spirit to sustain the spiritual lives of believers and help all of us to overcome the wiles of the enemy.

This blessing only comes by true belief in Jesus Christ and living a life according to God's Spirit! "For what the law could not do in that it was weak through the flesh, God did by sending His own Son in the likeness of sinful flesh, on account of sin: He condemned sin in the flesh, that the righteous requirement of the law might be fulfilled in us who do not walk according to the flesh but according to the Spirit" Romans 8:3-4 (NKJV). As Christians, we must realize _why_ God gave us His Son and a measure of Himself in the form of the Holy Spirit. It restores humankind back to Him. If we do not truly believe in Jesus and fail to live according to God's Spirit, *we will not be saved!* It is just that simple!

A Final Word from the Author

I realize that some will see this book as being a negative word and unexciting, but this truth must be told prior to the end of the age. Hopefully, it will alter and/or turn around someone's life for the better! Scripture clearly reveals that believers should be endowed with the Holy Spirit, become the temple of God, and regulate their life according to the Spirit. "All who are victorious will become pillars in the Temple of my God, and they will never have to leave it. And I will write on them the name of my God, and they will be citizens in the city of my God—the New Jerusalem that comes down from heaven from my God. And I will also write on them my new name" Revelation 3:12(NLT).

This must be accomplished soon in the lives of believers because our time is short *(according to the signs of the times)*. God's Spirit is the quintessential element of the Godhead that brings about the transformation of human flesh. Jesus and the Holy Spirit are the primary spiritual blessings sent from above to work on our behalf. They are the key elements in God's restoration plan for His creation *(see below):*

> *"Blessed be the God and Father of our Lord Jesus Christ, who has blessed us with every spiritual blessing in the heavenly places in Christ, just as He chose us in Him before the foundation of the world, that we should be holy and without blame before Him in love, having predestined us to adoption as sons by Jesus Christ to Himself, according to the good pleasure of His will, to the praise of the glory of His grace, by which He made us accepted in the Beloved" Ephesians 1:3-6 (NKJV).*

After Jesus ascended to the Father, God poured out His Spirit on believers for a Divine purpose. The purpose is to live a life according to the leading and guiding of God's Spirit as temples of God. As stated so many times in this book, if this is not done, we have not fulfilled God's purpose in His restoration process! The Holy Spirit changes the heart, mind, body and soul of those who believe in Jesus Christ and seek to become a witness in God's Kingdom.

John Elliott Williams

Made in the USA
Columbia, SC
15 March 2019